Hidden Glory

Incarnate God,
      lamp of my life,
displaying your divinity
in human flesh,

           reveal your light
           and clear my clouded mind.

Creative God,
      leaven of my spirit,
asserting your authority
in frail innocence,

           restore my vision
           and heal my distorted sight.

Redeeming God,
      Lord of my whole being,
exhibiting your power
in infant love,

           reclaim my hesitant faith
           so that, uncovering your glory
           for all to see,

I proclaim you
      light of my way,
and confess you to be
my Chosen One,

           now and always.

READ: Mark 1. 9 - 11

The heavens still open
the Spirit still descends.
Men and women still come to know
that they are the beloved Sons and Daughters of God.

'I just want you to know',
said a woman in Manchester,
'that my husband came home from church
a different man this morning'.

It was in Leeds that a woman said,
'I thought after my husband died
that I would never do anything, ever again, for anybody.
But God has spoken to me to-day
and I am going back to my home town
to take up the threads of my public life again'.

There was the young woman,
slightly spastic, who said,
'I think I am being called to be a minister
so that I can share the gospel
with other people like me'.

The Spirit still drives
people into the wilderness
to struggle with their call
and work out its implications.

'So far all my decisions and actions
have been made on the assumption
that I shall be a bank manager
for the rest of my working life.
Is that the call of God?
Or is it this nagging, persistent feeling
that I should serve him in some other way?
And if it is, and I said yes,
would it be fair to my family?'

The Baptism of Jesus

Jesus, you are the one
who rises from the water and the tomb
to offer new life to all.

> We offer our life
> as a sign of our worship.

Jesus, you are the one
who agrees to be baptised
to be at one with us.

> We offer our baptism
> as a sign of being with you.

Jesus, you are the one
for whom the heavens open
to allow the Spirit to descend.

> We offer our ready heart
> as a sign of our open life.

Jesus, you are the one
who is the Son so well loved
that God's delight is in you.

> We offer you our delight and joy
> as a sign of our everlasting love.

READ: Mark 1.14 - 20; Mark 3. 13 - 19;
Mark 9. 49 - 50

WEEK OF PRAYER FOR CHRISTIAN UNITY

'We now declare together our readiness
to commit ourselves to each other under God.
Our earnest desire is to become more fully,
in his own time,
the one Church of Christ,
united in faith, communion, pastoral care and mission.
Such unity is the gift of God.

With gratitude we have truly experienced this gift,
growing amongst us in these days.
We affirm our openness to this growing unity
in obedience to the word of God,
so that we may fully share,
hold in common and offer to the world
those gifts which we have received
and still hold in separation.
In the unity we seek
we recognise
that there will not be uniformity
but legitimate diversity.

It is our conviction that,
as a matter of policy
at all levels and in all places,
our churches must now move
from co-operation to clear commitment to each other,
in search of the unity for which Christ prayed
and in common evangelism and service of the world.'

From the Swanwick Declaration
which led to the creation of
the Council of Churches for Britain and Ireland (CCBI); Churches
Together in England (CTE); CYTUN (Churches Together in Wales)
and ACTS (Action of Churches Together in Scotland)

Friend of the People

Friend of the people,
you chose twelve
to be your friends and apostles.
    You chose us to be disciples
    to live in friendship with each other.

We are content to paddle
in the shallow water
unwilling to go deeper
in case we are overwhelmed;
not wanting to offend our neighbours
yet resisting compromise.

We skim the water
like a fisherman's float
unable to submerge ourselves fully;
not knowing what we will find
in the depths.

Call us from the comfort and safety
of our own ways,
to dare to deepen our friendship
with those who are different,
to find the bedrock of love,
beneath our insecurity.

Send us into deeper water
until with courage we immerse ourselves
and we see more clearly
different ways to strive
for a loving relationship
with our friends.

Friend of the people
you chose twelve
and made them apostles.
    You make us apostles
    to share your way with
    each other and the world.

READ: Mark 6. 30 - 44

I have been to Birmingham
where I saw homeless people
gathering together
for food and shelter
in a derelict church
converted by the living church
into a place where they could live and learn
and eat and sleep
and die with dignity.
>The cry of Jesus had been heard:
>'Give them something to eat yourselves'.

I have been to Nanjing
where I saw an awful orphanage
full of the sort of handicapped children
left over when all the others have been adopted.
Rows of babies in bare surrounds
would have been abandoned
to premature death
if the orphanage and its nurses
and UNICEF and AMITY
had not been there.
>They had heard the cry of Jesus:
>'Give them something to eat yourselves'.

I have been to Zambia
where I saw the bare brown earth
and heard the wail of mothers
wondering how they could fill their cooking pots
when mealie-meal gets so expensive
and cabbage has to be bought leaf by leaf.
And I passed by productive farms
with rich green fields and overflowing fruit:
living proof of what could be
>if more of us had heard the cry of Jesus:
>'Give them something to eat yourselves'.

Feeding of the 5000

Positive God,
why do I feel a negative figure in your plan?
It seems my belief is weak.
Why am I surprised when your plan works?
It happens again and again.
God of my life, forgive me.

Patient God,
why do I become a stumbling block?
I should be clearing the path, not blocking it.
Why am I sometimes an irritation in your plan
like a piece of grit in the eye, making things difficult?
God of my life, forgive me.

Caring God,
why do I think my body and mind are indestructible?
I should see the need to refresh my body, my soul and my mind.
Why do I waste so much time with minor difficulties?
I hide my eyes from the major ones.
God of my life, forgive me.

Mysterious God,
where are you?
Sometimes you are clearly there and I feel I could touch you.
Sometimes your way is clothed in a mist.
But within the mist I feel your presence.
God of my life, I thank you.

Providing God,
how can you feed us all?
My need is different from my neighbours'.
Yet your love provides what each of us requires,
and if I respond to your love, I am treated to a feast.
God of my life, I thank you.

READ: Mark 11. 15 - 17

Everywhere we went we saw
temples, churches and chapels
being built and re-built.

In a brick-making village outside Nanjing
the congregation had built their own church
from the bricks their hands had made.
In Shanghai there was a vast new auditorium
designed to seat 1,500 people
and a steeple built to touch the sky.

On an Ndola compound
a huge breeze block hangar
was the place where men and women worshipped God.
There were no seats, in fact no furniture at all.
The congregation brought their own
and took them home again.
At Tubalange, in the bush outside Lusaka,
there is just an empty site,
with concrete base
and a congregation saving up
till they can afford the materials
to make more bricks and build some more
until their church becomes a place of prayer.

At Milton Keynes a mighty city church grows up,
and Camberley's High Cross is beautiful and huge.
The tiny congregation at Fulbourn
have re-furbished and renewed
their delightful country chapel
for the service of their Lord;
while Stockwell Green, in Inner London,
sold their church and bought a shop
and made it a place of prayer.
At Yateley there is no building called a church at all,
but there is a people who are a church.

Jesus confronting the money-changers

"My temple will be called a house of prayer for the people of all nations - but you have turned it into a hideout for thieves".

It had nothing to do
with retreating from the world
to search for peace and quiet;
 - it had everything to do with
loving the Lord God
with heart and mind
and soul and strength.

It had nothing to do
with the bustle of business
in the courtyards of God's house;
 - it had everything to do
with finding and knowing God
at the heart of things.

Forgive us, Lord Jesus,
when we let fund-raising
get in the way of faith;
when we become so concerned
with the amount in the collection
we fail to see you at the centre
of our worship and our world.

Give us the determination
to tear down the tables of greed -
not only in our churches
but in our hearts as well;
help us to overturn
our materialistic attitudes
and offer ourselves,
wholly, in your service.

READ: Mark 13. 1 - 2; Mark 14.58

The church, like many other institutions,
was torn apart by the cultural revolution in China.
But when it was over the authorities
instituted a policy of religious freedom.
Since then church growth
as been startling and exhilarating.
Three church buildings have been
opened or re-opened
every two days.

City churches burst at the seams every Sunday,
spawning house groups and meeting points
in city and country.
Meetings for evangelism, study and prayer
are held regularly.
Young people are thronging into the Church
to join the old folk
who have kept the faith
through the decades of oppression.

Two million Bibles have rolled off
the Amity printing press outside Nanjing.

Christians are still a tiny minority
(around 1% of the population),
but Christianity is visible and growing
and its message influential.
Statistics for the number of Christians in China
are notoriously difficult to determine.
But informed guesses arrive at a figure
between 5 and 10 million.

We saw a brand new church in Shanghai
with congregations of 1000
at each of the two morning services
and village churches packed tight
with first generation Christians.

Living Temples

Nothing seemed more stable;
all marvelled at its magnificence;
many generations had helped to make it
a temple fit for you;

> *But you desired more.*

Today your love compels us
to see what you see:
temples made not by human hands,
but formed from human love.

God our Master Builder,
we confess that we have often followed our own plans, not yours:
> limiting you to our denominations,
> confining you within the structures of our buildings
> and restricting your presence to the times we choose to worship.

It is stable; it is comfortable.

> But you desire more.

You call us to leave our hand-made temples
to be where you are:
to be vulnerable, open and free.

So, overthrow our wilful ignorance;
bring down the walls of our indifference
to what the Church has become.

Then,
rescue us from the rubble,
fashion us into living stones,
and bind us together with the cement of your Spirit,
so that our whole lives can be made into temples fit for you.

READ: Mark 4. 1 - 20

I was privileged to offer the prayer of thanks
at each of the Thanksgiving Services
held for two of the great teachers of the church:
John Huxtable and Hubert Cunliffe-Jones,
who died during the year.

On behalf of us all
I gave thanks to God
that we had seen him in them.
I gave thanks for their love expressed as husbands and fathers,
for their friendship which crossed barriers
of intellect, outlook and nation,
for their careful counselling, ceaseless encouragement,
for their ability to break the bread of life
as they interpreted scripture,
for their letters and their prayers,
for their prophetic words
and political skills
which brought together churches, colleges and people,
for their gift of leading others
to faith in themselves, in others and in God,
for their gifts of intellect, training and study
which enabled them to lead others
into new pilgrimages of thought, experience and grace,
for their giving of themselves in ministry
in such a way that many were enabled
to see what it meant to minister.

The churches throughout the world
need teachers who can do for the next generation
what these men did for theirs.
Give thanks for them
and for those who are teachers of the church now.
Pray that God will raise up others
to do it in the future.

Teaching the Kingdom

Teach us, Jesus.

Teach us
> of sowers and shepherds,
> farmers and fools,
> camels and kings.

Teach us
> of your kingdom,
> hidden from sight,
> silent and secret,
> yet everywhere generously offered, freely given.

Forgive us
> our wasteful indifference to the clues of your kingdom,
> our shallow response to the challenge of your kingdom,
> our fickle digression from the way of your kingdom.

Find in us
> attention and ardour,
> depth and maturity
> sufficient to sow your living word.

Surprise us again
> with the increasing splendour
> and growing glory
> of your kingdom
> in us.

READ: Mark 2. 1 - 12

Because they have heard
that Jesus is present
they still break through the walls
that we have built
in order to bring for healing those who are hurt.

They built a wall in Belfast
and, with tragic irony,
called it the 'Peace Line'.
On each side of it
the Protestants and the Catholics gathered
thinking they could keep Jesus to themselves
and not let anyone else in.

But there are those who break through that wall: both ways.
Amongst them there are a group of men and women
who call themselves the Cornerstone Community.
They are Catholic and Protestant.
There are about twenty of them.
Five of them live in community
on the Springfield Road
right on the 'Peace Line'.

'We believe', they say, 'the very fact of our being together in West
Belfast is in itself a vital witness and resource in this area of almost total
polarisation; and together we seek to be channels of God's reconciling
love, sharing comfort, hope and reconciliation with those around us
through whatever joint initiatives or forms of support seem appropriate.'

We met a Catholic Priest, a Methodist Minister and a Quaker woman.
Whenever there is a killing amongst the Catholic community
they go together to that Catholic house to talk of the God
who is neither Catholic nor Protestant.
Whenever there is a killing amongst the Protestant community
they go together to that Protestant house to talk of the God
who is neither Protestant nor Catholic.

The Healer

The healer is at home, they said.
Hope soared
and then sank.

We know the feeling, Lord.
Life is overcrowded with casualties
looking for relief
and leaving little space for those who come last.
Waiting lists are long
and the healers overwhelmed.

Give us the hope that we can reach you,
> the faith that finds the way through
> and the space in which we can be with you.

They broke through the roof,
lowered him down,
paralysed.

We too are stiffened by fear
> and need you to release us;
overloaded with guilt
> and need you to lift it from us;
powerless to change
> and need you to take charge of us.

Help us to realise
> there are no limits to your love and power,
> nothing which you cannot heal and forgive.

Speak again the words, which set us on our feet.
Restore the self within us, and make us whole.
Free us to offer hands and hope to others
who need carrying to you.

READ: Mark 2. 13 - 17

Albert was a well known minister in Holland.
He was asked to conduct a major ecumenical service for Easter
in the largest church in Amsterdam.
He looked round for some way of trying to convey the thrill
and excitement of Resurrection.
He hit upon the idea of a trumpeter improvising
on the theme of Resurrection.
Improvisation was important: it was about rising from the dead.
He tried the major orchestra in the city
but the trumpeter there would not think of sinking
to improvisation.
So, on the advice of one of his younger church members,
he went to a night club and found a genius of a trumpeter.
The man agreed to play.

On Easter Sunday he did indeed play.
Starting from a low, groaning note he built it up to an almighty
crescendo of sound. They had never heard anything like it before.
It was moving, wonderful and magnificent.
Later that week Albert went round to pay the man.
'Who were those people in church on Sunday?', the man asked,
'Unlike the people here, they listend,
they appreciated, they understood.'
Albert explained that these were the people of God at worship.
'Tell me more', said the man,
'I don't know anything about all this.'
They met three or four times.
They talked about the Gospel, about God and about Jesus,
they talked about the promises and the demands of God.
'I think I would like to be baptised', said the man.

Albert told the story to the Elders meeting.
'Wonderful', they said,
'But he will stop playing his trumpet in that nasty night club,
won't he?'

Jesus, friend of outcasts

Jesus, what do I do?
I know my ways were not always
honest or trustworthy
that I cheated a bit sometimes
but I've put all that behind me now.
I came when you called
and I'll try my best
to do things your way.
But its my friends!

Jesus, what do I do about my friends?
I can hear the mutterings behind my back.
The teachers of the law say you shouldn't be here
eating with me and my friends.
Virtuous people call them sinners
 - they never wear the right clothes
 - they have no job or do the wrong one.
But I can't throw them out. They're my friends!

Jesus, forgive me if I'm wrong
if they shouldn't be here.
But they wanted to meet you too.
You didn't go away when they came in
you sat at the same table
ate the same bread
drank the same wine.
Does that mean that despite their faults
you'll be their friend too?

Jesus said: "I came not to call the virtuous but sinners".

READ: Mark 1. 12 - 13; Mark 9. 33 - 49

Alone, all alone,
One hundred and seventy six days,
One hundred and seventy six nights,
In solitary confinement,
Alone, all alone.

Perhaps like God on the day of creation,
Alone, all alone,
Perhaps like an animal inside the cage,
Alone, all alone.

Isolated and thinking,
Alone, all alone,
Dreaming and suffering nightmares,
Alone, all alone,
Cut off from the world of human beings,
And brought closer to the world of lions and mabas.

No visits from my beloved, beloved ones,
Alone, all alone,
Neither Bishop nor Bible allowed in,
Alone, all alone.

No music, not even from the Police Brass Band,
No mirror permitted to create my twinself,
And conquer the lonliness,
Alone, all alone.

Alone in a solitary cell alone,
Alone in a solitary corner alone,
Alone in solitary confusion alone,
Alone in solitary conversation alone,
Yes, alone in solitary combat,
Against solitary confinement,
Alone, all alone.

A musical poem written and sung by a young South African detainee.
We heard him sing it in Speyer, Germany during a 'Bread for the
World' event.

Tempted

Son of God,
>driven by the Spirit, tempted by Satan,
>befriended by animals, helped by angels,
>>like us you were tried and tested,
>>>**purify us;**
>for us you kept the faith,
>>>**purify us;**
>with us you became our strength,
>>>**purify us.**

Children of God,
>led astray by our arrogance,
>perverted by our pride,
>abused by our selfishness,
>>when through sin we destroy your innocence,
>>>**forgive us;**
>>when through cynicism we destroy your faith,
>>>**forgive us;**
>>when through pride we destroy your confidence,
>>>**forgive us.**

Son of God,
>take our hands that put work before all else,
>take our feet that walk the way of ambition,
>take our eyes that greed blinds to others' needs,
>>and nail them to the cross,
>>until temptation loses its hold on us,
>>and we are purified and forgiven.
>>>**Amen.**

READ: Mark 3. 20 - 35

'Whoever does the will of God is my brother.'

He, with four others, had started the church
in the village outside Hanzhou in 1980.
Now, ten years later, there were 700 worshippers.
They visited the sick, helped with flood relief,
helped to organise village festivities, had planned families,
contributed to the peace, the security and the environment of the village.
They had built a new church and hoped to build another across the river.
His eyes shone.
'What problems do you have?' I asked
'We have no problems', he replied.

'Whoever does the will of God is my sister.'

She was about fifteen years old, one of the extended family.
She did a great deal of the cooking in the house in Lusaka.
When our hostess was out at work,
the girl looked to our comfort and ease.
Anxious to please without being servile.
On the Saturday night the whole family was gathered
along with us, their guests.
Into the room came the girl carrying a pile of Bibles.
She distributed them, conducted a Bible Study
and then asked me, 'Anything to add?'
There was nothing to add.

'Whoever does the will of God is my mother.'

She showed us round the most sophisticated institution
for the care of the elderly and the mentally handicapped.
It was in Landau, Germany, and run by the church.
She introduced us to her sister, one of the mentally handicapped patients.
'We had to hide her when we were small and the Nazis were in power,
but now I can be with her all the time and introduce her to our guests.'

Family likeness

You bore me in pain, mother,
in sweat and squalor
in a steamy outhouse
on the straw.

You nurtured me in love, mother,
taught me to care
for my brothers and sisters -
and my heavenly Father too.

Surely you must recognise
that I have other mothers,
other sisters and brothers
whose family resemblance
is so striking
you know at once
who is their Father.

Some say the Prince
of devils spawned me
and gives me the power
to heal and save.
Let them look at my deeds
and listen to my words.
Am I not still about my Father's business?

God, our mother, father, sister, brother,
help us to recognise
other members of your extended family.
May we see the likeness to Jesus in each other
and may we grow more like him every day.

READ: Mark 8. 31 - 9. 1

Jothi's story: from Papua New Guinea

The MENDULI shops which are run by
the United Church of Papua New Guinea and the Solomon Islands
were burnt to the ground.
The person responsible for the fire was a Menduli employee.
He was trying to light the gas stove but could not find a match
and whilst searching he left the gas on.
On his return he struck the match and you can guess what happened.
There was a big bang and in no time the buildings caught fire.
People quickly gathered around the place
and police tried their best to put out the fire.
Meanwhile the bystanders, including some police,
took the opportunity to loot the stores nearby.
They took whatever they could lay their hands on!

When I heard this, I felt like crying.
Because Menduli has done a lot and is still doing a lot
to improve the province and serve the community.
Here people and police are looting the goods instead of protecting them.

I am sure you will be sad to hear that I was attacked by a person
one evening when I was on my way to church.
He did not harm me, but only took my bilum
which contained a bible and hymn book.
The guy must have thought I had plenty of money.
Poor like me, where will I get money to put in a bilum?
My prayer for him is that the bible he has stolen will speak to him.
Perhaps he may give his life to God.

Jothi Dasappa is a member of the Church of South India.
She serves as a missionary in Papua New Guinea.

Jesus speaks of his suffering and death

Jesus the Christ,
you challenge us
not as spectators
but as friends:
'Who do you say I am?'

Jesus, the friend,
you trust us
with your secret:
that to live by love
is the way to suffering and pain.

Jesus, the man,
you fear us
as we try to persuade
both you and ourselves
that there must be a more comfortable way.

Jesus, the life,
you call us
to follow you
by taking up our cross
and witness to your painful peace.

Jesus, the Lord,
you are in us:
in your suffering
you meet our pain,
our deepest fears and weakness.

Free us, then,
from the anxieties that make us shrink
from being what you have called us to be:
your followers and friends.

READ: Mark 12. 37b - 44

I do not know very much about her story.
I know she is a widow.
She comes to stay at the Centre
from time to time.

I know she has a son
who was a missionary
in the Far East,
until he came home
to take up his ministry
in England.

One day at the Centre,
she asked
if we would take her
to the induction
of the new minister
at the church in the next town.
Of course we would, and did.
But why this interest
in this particular minister?
'Oh, she was one of my Rangers
in the company I used to run years ago'.

Some widow, some mite!

Two ministers that I know of,
and how many other
women and men
in the church and the world
have been touched by that one life?

How many more widows
have given more
than all those who give to the treasury?

The Widow's Prayer

Oh dear, Lord, I wish I had more to give.
I almost feel I have no right to be here at all, in this beautiful place
where you are worshipped and your word is spoken.
Look at these clothes - I feel ashamed to come to church in them.
Of course, I know I've as much right really as anyone, they tell me so.
But it makes me nervous being here among these people
who are so confident about it all.

There's that nice solicitor,
such a charming, polite man and always so immaculate.
       I must say, though, I had a shock when I got his bill
       for dealing with Arthur's will.

And the doctor's wife: what a lot of good work she does in the community.
I wish I had an ounce of her talent. Her family doesn't suffer either.
They'll be off for a good hotel lunch after service, and then drive to the
seaside for the afternoon.
       Of course, we could never have afforded that.

Then there's the minister - what a gifted man!
How fortunate we are to have him.
       If only I was bright enough
       to understand all those deep things he tells us.

Real leaders they are, all of them.
They give so much in every way to keep the cause going.
And here I am with nothing to offer but a couple of coins
in the bottom of my purse. I feel terrible about this, Lord.
This wouldn't even buy me a cup of tea, so heaven only knows what *you*
can do with it. But its a long time to pension day.
Ah well, here goes, while no one's looking - drop it in the box.

Our Prayer

Lord Jesus, thank you for pointing out an anonymous woman
to show us that the cost of your kingdom is counted in pennies.
Teach us now to trade in our status for a pennyworth of service,
      our comfort for a pennyworth of commitment,
      our righteousness for a pennyworth of repentance,
and to offer it all in the treasury of eternal life.

The Passion of Christ is not simply re-enacted
in ecclesiastical ritual at Communion Table or Altar.
It is a drama acted and re-enacted through the whole of time
and its stage is the world.

What a year it was:
the rape of Kuwait, the war in the Gulf,
the deaths of 100,000 - 200,000 people,
the burning of a thousand wells,
a desert left to blow away in the wind;
the slaughter of the Shi'ites, the killing of the Kurds,
their flight to the hills, 2000 deaths every day;
twenty-seven million people facing starvation
in Ethiopia, Sudan, Angola, and Mozamibique,
forgotten because the television cameras were elsewhere;
cholera in South America, fighting in South Africa,
suppression in Estonia and Latvia,
teenagers and taxi drivers butchered in Belfast.

So God's heart is broken still.
Still his blood is poured out onto the streets of Iraq
and down the valleys that run from Turkey and Iran.
It is his lips that lie parched
on the empty breasts of grieving mothers all over Africa.
It is his cholera infested body that lies dying in Chile and Peru.
It is his mother that weeps in Belfast
and cries out that revenge should not be sought.

We despised them and held them of no account,
objects from which people turn away their eyes.
Yet it is our afflictions they are bearing,
our pain they endure.

Why only them?
Aren't both the suffering and the triumph of God
to be shared by us all?

Lord of the Cross

Handed over, condemned, mocked,
spat upon, flogged, killed,
yet risen and alive, and with us now.
> **Lord of the Cross we praise you**
> **and glory in your life, broken and given for all.**

We hold back from the world in confusion or fear,
but you journey on into the heart of human cruelty
pain, hatred and agony.
> **Lord of the Cross we praise you**
> **and glory in your life, broken and given for all.**

We hope for glory in heaven above
and look for good seats for us and ours,
but you show your glory in the world as it is
nailed between two robbers.
> **Lord of the Cross we praise you**
> **and glory in your life, broken and given for all.**

We aim for cheap glory and undeserved rewards,
but you drink the cup of suffering, drain its bitter dregs
and enter the depths of loneliness and death.
> **Lord of the Cross we praise you**
> **and glory in your life, broken and given for all.**

We make easy promises of loyalty
and speak brave but empty words,
but you promise us a share in your life.
> **Lord of the Cross we praise you**
> **and glory in your life, broken and given for all.**

We compare ourselves with others and look for status and approval,
but you kneel and serve, bowing like a slave,
dying like a criminal and setting us free for life.
> **Lord of the Cross we praise you**
> **and glory in your life, broken and given for all.**

Sunday   Mark 11.1-11   Jesus in Triumph

King of the universe, whose son entered Jerusalem riding on a donkey to the praise of the crowds, help us to recognise in him the one who comes in the name of the Lord, and to acclaim him, crying 'Hosanna in the highest! 'May we make sacrifices for the coming of your kingdom, giving not only our hallelujah, but also our hearts.

Monday   Mark 14.32-52   Jesus in Gethsemane

Abba, Father, whose son went through agony of soul in Gethsemane and betrayal by his friends, we marvel at the torment and the horror of knowing what his calling meant. We pray that we may be awakened from indifference to share his struggle, and that we may neither betray him with a kiss, nor flee from him naked, but stand by him in his hour of need.

Tuesday   Mark 14.53-65   Jesus before the High Priest

Great High Priest, who stood before the chief priest and scribes and heard their false testimony and their blasphemy, only to be condemned yourself for blasphemy, help us to bear clear witness to the truth in you, unobscured by our prejudices. We ask it for the honour of your name: you are the one who sits at the right hand of God, and will come with clouds of glory.

Wednesday   Mark 14.66-72   Jesus denied by Peter

Jesus Christ, master and friend, who warned your disciple Peter that he would deny you, give us the grace not to fear being unmasked as your friends. When we weep at our inconstancy, restore us as you restored him. Use us in your service, for the sake of your name which may not be denied.

Thursday   Mark 15.1-20   Jesus condemned and mocked

Mighty God, source of all power, whose son was condemned by Pilate and mocked by soldiers, we ask blessing and mercy on all who wield power or authority, however great or small, that they may exercise it with justice, humility and respect, so that when in their turn they stand before your justice, they may know your love.

Friday   Mark 15.21-41   Jesus dies on the cross

Father of our Lord Jesus Christ, who heard his cry of desolation upon the cross and tore the veil of separation in two, have mercy on us in our deepest need, and grant that, through the man who was Son of God, we may come close to you and stand alongside all humanity in its despair.

Saturday   Mark 15.42-67   Jesus in the tomb

Jesus, whose body was laid in a tomb by Joseph of Arimathea and cared for by the two Marys, help us, men and women, to care for others in their hour of helplessness and so to serve you. Stay with us as evening approaches, and in the hour of our death care for us.

It was Easter Sunday in Blackpool.
After the service he came up to me
and asked if I would like to see his workshop.
It was there, in a cellar under the church.
Along one side, boxes of rusty tools,
down the middle a work bench,
and the other side: boxes and boxes of shining, sharp tools.
He and his family were committed to 'Tools for Self-Reliance'.
All their spare time was spent in
collecting, cleaning, sharpening, painting old tools
to be sent to parts of the world
where the lack of tools
prevented skilled people from earning their living.

It turned out that I was to have lunch with them.
During the meal he said,
'I quite enjoyed the service this morning,
but I wish you hadn't used that prayer'.

I had used that prayer of Alan Gaunt's:
'We look for the day when the maimed will run,
fools will be wise,
the insane of sound mind.
Politicians will make peace
and feed the people
and turn tanks into combine harvesters'.

'It was that line', he said,
'the one about turning tanks in combine harvesters,
after that I spent the whole service
working out how to do it!'

He is going ahead of you
into Galilee
and into Blackpool.

Confession ... of faith?

I confess, Lord,

I am worried, puzzled and alarmed!
>It worries me that there is no Easter joy,
>no hope or faith for the women.
>It puzzles me that the Gospel can end
>with terrified and tongue-tied people.
>It alarms me that there is no good news,
>so how can I believe in resurrection?

I confess, Lord,

I have much in common with the three women!
>I approach the tomb
>full of questions, doubts and fears.
>I panic when confronted
>by strange events I cannot explain.
>I run away
>frightened and refuse to talk about it.

Help me, Lord.

Lift up my eyes
>to see the obstacles rolled away.

Encourage me
>to enter the unknown with faith.

Send me
>to find you again in the familiar.

Meet me
>even when I run away.

Listen to me
>in my silent distress, and

bring me
>through terror to trust.

Lord, I believe. Help my unbelief.

READ: Mark 16. 9 - 13

...when they were told that that he was alive
and that she had seen him
they did not believe it.

A story from Taiwan:

The New Century Woman was the topic of the sixth annual conference
of the Taiwan Association of Theologically Trained Women.
Nineteen women participated.

First they came to realize that there are many levels of oppression
facing women in the developing world.
The women began to open up and share their own stories.
This sharing of self continued late into the night.
The women's pain and tears experienced in their ministries
were given voice.
Participants were consoled by their sisters.

Then it was suggested that after breaking down the oppression of silence
and speaking out about the pain and injustice they had been suffering,
then the next step was to make connections.
A spiritual connection with God
enables one to understand her life, her world, her calling.
Making connections with the foremothers of the past,
one learns and draws courage and strength
from their struggles and experience.

The reality is that Taiwanese women do share
their stories, pain and struggles.
But their significance is usually minimized
by using the term 'gossip',
and they are kept within the circle of women.
Their experiences are shrugged off as 'our fate'.
These suppressions become silent sins
which infect every aspect of human life and social structure,
generation after generation.

Too good to be true

Lord, our minds are full of questions,
and like the disciples we dare not believe you are alive.
Who did Mary Magdalene see on that first morning,
and how could she recognise you
after the scourging and wounding,
the nakedness and shame,
the cruel crucifixion?
Are you really alive?
It is too good to be true.

Lord, we know what death is like.
We see it on our television screens in casual violence,
or coming slowly to those who die of hunger in far-off places.
We see it when it happens to a friend,
or closer still to one we love.
We know the pain of separation, the emptiness, the loss,
the sorrow of mourning, the tears, the heart-brokenness.
Are you really alive?
It is too good to be true.

Lord, two of your friends said they met you
as they walked along the road,
although you appeared in another form.
How did they know you then,
and what form did you take?
Do you speak to each of us in a different way,
as we share your word,
or break bread together at your table?
Is this too good to be true?

Lord you were not seen by Caiaphas, or Pilate, or the crowd.
You would not compel belief.
If you have ears, you said, then hear.
If you have eyes, then see.
See my works and follow me.
And to those who listen, who see, who try to follow,
you give your own abundant life,
life that is not destroyed by death.
Good enough to be true!

READ: Mark 12. 18 - 27

A funeral address for an unknown person

I do not know...
but you do.
You are sons and daughters, husband/wife.
You are friends, neighbours, colleagues.
That fact that you are here
is an indication that.....'s life made some impact on yours.
It may be that his/her love taught you how to love,
his/her set of values enabled you to arrive at yours,
his/her strength upheld you through tough times,
his/her gentleness defused your anger time and again,
his/her sense of humour taught you what you could laugh at.
I do not know; but you do.
The fact is that if....... had not lived,
if he/she had not lived when he/she did,
if he/she had not lived in the way that he/she did,
to some extent your life would be different.

The Gospel does not tell us much about life after death,
it uses a different expression: 'eternal life'.
That means that when we have seen Jesus
and the quality of his life,
we have seen the sort of life that death cannot touch.
That quality of life is always at home with God.

If in the life of ......
you have seen any of the qualities
you have seen in Jesus,
you have seen
in your home, your street, your family, your circle of friends,
someone who already had the marks of life that is eternal,
that death cannot touch, that is at home with God.

If that is so do not mourn for him/her:
mourn for yourselves, for you are the ones who have lost.

God of the Living

I am curious,
what will heaven be like?
Does Peter guard the pearly gates?
Who will be there and how will I recognise them?
Have dogs and cats a heaven of their own?

Lord, are my questions as absurd as the one the Sadducees asked?
They were curious to see if you could be tricked by their questions.
You answered them in their own kind and then went on to proclaim

> **God is not God of the dead,**
> **but God of the living.**

You say the same words to me.
Help me to put aside my curiosity about the next life and live
in this one. Help me to put my trust in the power of him who
raised you from the dead.

O God of the living I want to be alive!

Let me die with Christ that I might live with him.
Let me be dead to sin and alive to you.

O God of the living I want to be alive!

Let me die to self that I might live for others.
Let me be dead to falsehood that I might live the truth.

O God of the living I want to be alive!

Let me die to my failures that I might live to honour you.
Let me be dead to my past that I might live in the present.

O God of the living I want to be alive!

READ: Mark 1. 21 - 28

A story from Myanmar (Burma)

Standing by its very name,
the Church-run Agape Clinic at Tahan town, Myanmar,
completed its first year of service
by diligently serving rural poor and disadvantaged people
with the love of Christ
and gave medical treatment to more than 28,300 patients
(perhaps 12,148 individuals)
which is an average of 105.6 patients on any working day!

Thanks to overseas partners (CWM)
the clinic had a good start on 1st April 1989
with basic needs of equipment
and laboratory facilities and other instruments
purchased from donations
which enable the Clinic
to levy minimum service charges to patients
and to sell medicines
at lower prices than local drug stores.

We had expected to have an X-ray machine
before the end of 1989,
but it is still now a matter of months
before it can be installed at the Clinic.
It is lamentable indeed to say that right now (*Summer 1990*)
not less than 30,000 people in Kale and Kabaw
are without any X-ray facility.

I am now hopeful that we can bring in the equipment
within the next two months
and with the X-ray facility at our disposal,
we have decided to have an additional doctor
who will be responsible for surgical cases.

Presbyterian Church of Myanmar

Who are you Jesus?

Who are you Jesus,
that you speak with such authority?
Not like scholars and teachers,
simply repeating each other,
you speak the Word of God
to us and all who will listen.
>The power of God living within you
>shines through everything you say.

>>Lord Jesus, help us
>>>to hear what you are saying.
>>>to understand what you are teaching,
>>>to know God's power in our lives
>>>and in the words we speak of you.

Who are you Jesus,
that you act with such authority?
Never allowing evil
to go unchallenged,
you release the possessed,
healing in the Father's name.
>The power of God living within you
>shines through everything you do.

>>Lord Jesus, help us
>>>to see what you are doing,
>>>to understand where evil exists,
>>>to know God's power living in us
>>>as we seek to bring your healing.

Jesus, recognised by the spirits,
allow us to recognise who you really are,
allow us always to be amazed
at your power, your goodness,
your mercy and your grace,
for you truly are the Son of God.

READ: Mark 3. 1 - 6

'Do you have healing services in your church?'

'In our church every service is a healing service!'

'What do you mean?'

'We are conscious that the whole purpose of our worship
is to pay attention to God.
The prayers we say, the hymns we sing, the scriptures we read,
the word that comes alive in the preaching,
all pierce the shell of indifference and self concern
that we create around us to keep out God.
The silences allow us to float in God's presence
and be upheld by it
like bathers in the Dead Sea.
The sacraments allow us to touch
and to be touched by God.
When the minister holds a baby in her arms
or stands in the pool and holds a believer
and uses water as a sign of the new life
that is beginning in them,
so we are reminded
that we are forever held in the arms of God
and surrounded by a love that never lets us go.
As bread is broken at the Table
and wine is poured out,
we remember the one
whose body is broken and whose blood is spilled for us,
and he is closer to us than breathing
and nearer than hands and feet.

Anger, despair, resentment, and bitterness
are burnt up like mist in the morning sun,
hurt and pain are wrapped in love,
and we are born again, made whole,
and given new life.'

Release

All seeing God,
>you know the inner thoughts
>that paralyse our lives,
>the stubbornness which creates prison bars,
>the chains of convention holding us down
>so that we fail to grasp
>the essential need
>to be made whole
>by you.

>>**Lord, help us to see
>>and know our need.**

Sorrowing God,
>take us by the hand
>and lead us away from
>believing that we know best
>and insisting on what we want.
>Take us to the point
>where we can see
>how to help
>and not harm.

>>**Lord, help us to accept
>>and know your way.**

Forgiving God,
>release us from everything that withers our spirit and
>binds our lives.
>Break down the restricting bars and chains
>with your redeeming love,
>so that with confidence we may
>obey your son's command
>to step forward
>stretch out our hands
>and know that we are healed.

>>**Lord, help us to experience
>>and know your healing power.**

READ: Mark 4. 35 - 41

They took us out to the saltings
at Tollesbury on the Blackwater Estuary.
The view was dominated
by the dark red lightship
tied up at the pier way out in the marsh.
It was the latest acquisition
of a group called *Fellowship Afloat.*

Starting with the vision
of a couple of Christians
this group first bought a small fishing smack,
then an old Thames sailing barge,
and now the lightship.
They also have a number of sailing dinghies
as well as canoes.

What is *Fellowship Afloat?*
'It is living and working together;
it is learning to sail in each other's company;
it is the hiss of Tilly lamps and voices singing to a guitar;
it is time to sit and stare at salt marsh, sea and boats -
and time to listen;
it is an opportunity to realise that God is interested in each person;
it is learning that God is real and that he is here -
not just in church, but out on the water,
in the boat.
He is where we are.'

That experience was given at first to church-based young people only.
But later came groups of young people with damaged lives,
sent by social workers and probation officers,
who, in a boat, surrounded by wind and waves,
came to realise their dependence on each other
and on God.

Do you not care?

Wake up, wake up
we need you.
Why do you sleep when we call?

Teacher, we are sinking!
We are battered by the demands of living.
The children learn to fight in the streets,
the young people abuse their bodies with drugs,
each cigarette we smoke is a heart beat less
and we drown our fear with the amount we drink.

Teacher, we are sinking!
The world you made to rise with you
drowns deeper still with every year.
Arms are made and sold to create new wealth
and then are used to destroy the earth;
forests are burned, and deserts blow away in the wind.

Wake up, wake up,
stretch out your hands again
in power and in compassion.
Command the peace
that will still our fears,
rebuke our sins,
renew our trust in you
and fill our hearts once more with wonder and with awe.
Travel with us
through storm and stillness
doubt and faith,
death and life.

Show us, once more, that you are Lord of all.

READ: Mark 16. 14 - 19 & Mark 14. 61b - 62

Remember the God
who is both creator of the world
and is a creature of it.

Remember the God who
brought the earth in being,
was Father and Mother to it,
yet entered into human life through a mother's womb;
who laid the earth's foundations
and set its corner stones in place,
yet learned to measure wood in a carpenter's workshop;
who supported the sea at its birth and established its bounds,
yet sailed on a lake in fishermens' boats;
who sent the dawn to its post and assigned the morning its place,
yet knew the tiredness of night
and the refreshment of daybreak;
who clothed the earth with green
and made grass spring up on thirsty ground,
yet walked in desert places and was thirsty himself;
who provided food for all the earth,
yet was hungry himself;
who is the judge of all the earth,
yet was the victim of its injustice;
who gave the world its life,
yet allowed the world to murder him.

Our God is Lord of all the earth,
and is the victim of it.

Lift up to God the earth,
that its fabric, torn by human hands,
may be repaired.
Lift up to God the peoples
that their communities, destroyed by human greed,
may be restored.

Ascension

Jesus, Lord,
Son of Man and Son of God,
seated at the right hand of the Father,

> **we worship and adore you,**
> **we acknowledge you to be the Lord.**

Jesus, Lord, Messiah,
Son of the blessed God
by whose Word all was created,

> **we worship and adore you,**
> **for all things have their being in you.**

Jesus, Lord, set free from the bounds of time and space,
living Lord, bidding us go everywhere
and preach your saving love,

> **we worship and adore you,**
> **come and be Lord of your Church.**

You came to your disciples and rebuked them,
they wouldn't listen to the women
who knew they had seen you alive.
We, too, are stubborn and faithless
we brush aside the experience of others
because it is not like our own.
Forgive us for seeking to contain you
in the little boxes we have made:
structures, procedures and traditions

Jesus, Lord,
Son of Man and Son of God,
seated at the right hand of the Father,

> **have mercy on us.**
> **Come and be Lord of your Church.**
> **Come and be Lord of my life.**

READ: Mark 1. 8; Mark 14. 28; Mark 16. 20

The story of Bishop Lesie Boseto of the Solomon Islands

I am known as a 'grass-roots Bishop'.
I am not a 'grass-skirt Bishop'.
There is a difference!
The former has living roots,
so that it represents life.
The latter has no life
because it has already been uprooted from the earth.
I like the name they call me
because I want to be more with the people at grass-roots
in order to develop grass-root theology
and lay people's participation in church,
local communities and our national life.

God created this earth.
His presence is everywhere.
Before, I used to believe that God's Spirit can only be given
at the theological colleges, Bible colleges and universities
in England, Rome, Canada, USA etc.

But now I have discovered
that our true God, the Father,
stands amongst us in his risen life
and directly asks us in our local languages
(not in English, or Greek, or French or Spanish)
the question, namely:
'Solomon Islanders, who do you say I am?'

This discovery helps me
to express in theological terms
the reality of Christ on our own soil.
We can only love the Christ
we recognise living in our midst,
who is prepared to struggle with us.

Come, Holy Spirit

Come, Holy Spirit:

cleansing power of God

forgive and heal us,

purging fire of God

forgive and heal us,

purifying spirit of God

forgive and heal us;

leaping power of God

direct and lead us,

dancing fire of God

direct and lead us,

enlivening spirit of God

direct and lead us;

burning power of God

enthuse and empower us,

warming fire of God

enthuse and empower us,

comforting spirit of God

enthuse and empower us;

**creative power of God,
searing fire of God,
Holy Spirit of God,**

COME TO US NOW!

**Set us on fire for Jesus
as we light up the world for him.**

READ: Mark 1. 10 - 11; Mark 14. 22 - 26

We were taken into a classroom in Zambia.
It was obvious that the class had been studying geometry.
There, on the wall, was a chart
all about the properties of angles.
But unfortunately all the way through the chart
the teacher had mis-spelt the word 'angle';
instead he or she had written 'angel'.

So we discovered that:

90 degrees makes one right angel!

if the angle is less than 90 degrees
that is an acute angel!

if the angle is greater than 90 degrees
that is an obtuse angel!

and then, at the bottom of the chart, it read
'and two right angels make half a revolution'!

That happy accident reminded me
that there is some relationship between angels,
messengers of God,
those on whom the Spirit rests,
those who are the body of Christ,
and revolutions
in the church,
in the community,
and in the world.

God takes delight
in those who are his sons and daughters.
He will drink the fruit of the vine again
when they, with him, have enabled the Kingdom of God to be seen.

God's break-through

God, creator of all that is,
you broke the chaos that reigned over all things
and brought the heavens and the earth into being.

God, creator of all that is,
you broke the silence of the heavens and spoke
as you poured out your Spirit on your Son.

Jesus Christ, Son of God,
you broke the bread, and then your body,
to reveal God's heart deep within you.

Jesus Christ, Son of God,
you poured the wine and spilt the blood
to reveal the Spirit flowing from you.

Spirit of God, flowing freely,
you broke the bars which imprisoned believers
to set them free to walk with the Father and the Son.

Spirit of God, flowing freely,
you broke the chains which bound the nations
to release the earth to breath your freedom.

Creator God,
Father, Son and Spirit,
break again chaos's anger and heavens' silence,
break again your body and spill your blood,
break again all that hinders the freedom of your people.
Let your Spirit speak
of your Son's sacrifice
and of your Father's love.

READ: Mark 2. 23 - 28

When we were in Speyer,
visiting the Church of the Palatinate,
they arranged that we should be shown round the town.
They took us to the Jewish quarter
and showed us some of the ancient buildings.
What moved us most
was to be taken down the steps,
to an ancient pool
which was used
for ritual washing
after times of uncleanliness.

It was important that such pools
were of living water.
That is, not still water
for still water becomes stagnant
and unable to cleanse.

They told us how,
in medieval times,
the plague had come to Speyer.
The Jews, who kept themselves ritually clean,
were kept free of the plague.
The rest of the population,
to whom such rituals were foreign,
caught the plague and died.

So great was the difference
between the two communities,
that they thought
the Jews must be poisoning their wells,
and so they persecuted them.

Ritual washing was made for men and women,
not men and women for ritual washing.

This is the Day

Lord of the Sabbath,
your liberated love is not bound by rigid rules;
your free spirit is not quenched by the letter of the law.
For you, every day is wholesome as wheat, holy as bread.
So we offer you everything we do today:
>> at work, at rest, in public praise and in private prayer:
>>> This is the day that the Lord has made.
>>> **We will rejoice and be glad in it.**

We ask your blessing
on those who must work today for our safety and security.
Be where they are, and in what they do.
>> Let them say with us:
>>> This is the day that the Lord has made.
>>> **We will work and be busy in it.**

We ask your blessing
on those who will rest today after a hard working week.
Let them find time for relaxation,
better to face the demands of tomorrow.
>> Let them say with us:
>>> This is the day that the Lord has made.
>>> **We will rest and be refreshed in it.**

We ask your blessing
on all your people gathered today to worship you.
Tune our praise to your glory,
and our prayers to the pangs of your hungry world.
Equip us to see and serve you tomorrow
in the places where we live and work.
>> So shall we proclaim with all your creation:
>>> This is the day that the Lord has made.
>>> **We will rejoice and be glad in it.**

Lord of the Sabbath,
let this and all our days be wholesome and holy to you,
for you are the same
yesterday, today and for ever.

READ: Mark 5. 21 - 43

A story from Japan

Yodagawa Christian Hospital in Osaka
operates a hospice programme on the top floor.
The purpose of the hospice is
to provide supportive care to the dying
with 'hands rather than machines.'

Life-prolonging measures are not used,
but patients' physical pains are alleviated
through adequate medication.
Emotional support is given by a team
which includes pastors and social workers.
The average length of stay for patients is fifty days
and patients' ages range from thirty to over ninety.
Most of them have terminal cancer.

The ward has an adjacent rooftop Japanese garden
where green trees and a fish pond provide
the three elements of happiness in Japanese culture:
green, water and fish.
The staff spend much time talking with the patients.
They sit beside the bed rather than stand
so that eye level contact will signify equality
and also to show that they are happy
to spend time with patients.

The Japanese word for healing
literally means 'laying hands on'
and the staff make efforts to have physical contact
as much as possible - through a touch or a hug - with the patients.

Families are encouraged to visit frequently.
They are also encouraged to bring along children,
who often are the most effective pain-relievers.

Christ is our confidence

The Woman

Christ you are our confidence.
I come to you
hoping, yet afraid.
Afraid to acknowledge
my need before others,
I try secretly to touch your cloak.
I feel better,
but, to my dismay,
what I feared has happened.
You demand that I should openly confess.
I kneel.
My shame, my hurt,
is seen by all.
In that openness
is your healing.
Your peace is mine.
                    Christ you are my confidence.

Jairus

Christ you are our confidence.
I come to you
asking help for one I love.
Suddenly I'm made aware
of someone else's claim to your attention.
Must my loved one wait
while some unknown person's prayer is answered?
Fear for my loved one's life engulfs me.
Then comes your assurance,
'Don't be afraid.'
Doubt and despair leave.
Quietly within our home
your presence brings new life.
My loved one lives.
                    Christ you are my confidence.

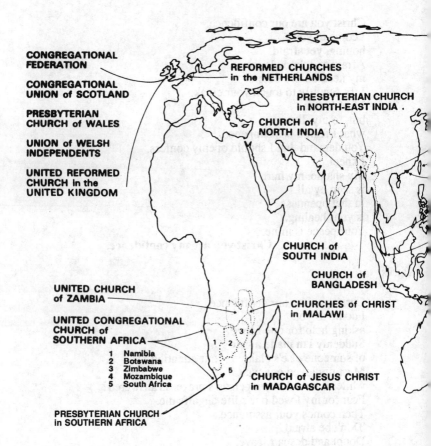

CONGREGATIONAL FEDERATION

CONGREGATIONAL UNION of SCOTLAND

PRESBYTERIAN CHURCH of WALES

UNION of WELSH INDEPENDENTS

UNITED REFORMED CHURCH in the UNITED KINGDOM

REFORMED CHURCHES in the NETHERLANDS

PRESBYTERIAN CHURCH in NORTH-EAST INDIA

CHURCH of NORTH INDIA

CHURCH of SOUTH INDIA

CHURCH of BANGLADESH

UNITED CHURCH of ZAMBIA

UNITED CONGREGATIONAL CHURCH of SOUTHERN AFRICA

1 Namibia
2 Botswana
3 Zimbabwe
4 Mozambique
5 South Africa

CHURCHES of CHRIST in MALAWI

CHURCH of JESUS CHRIST in MADAGASCAR

PRESBYTERIAN CHURCH in SOUTHERN AFRICA

of the COUNCIL FO

CHURCHES

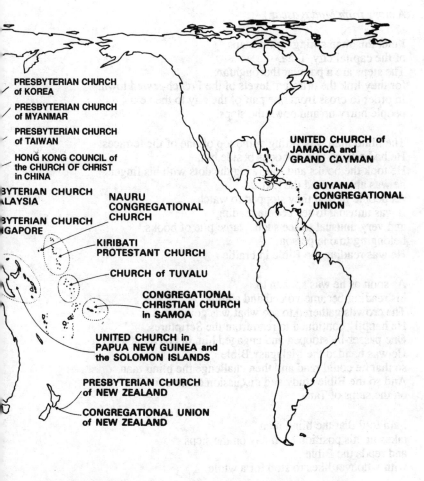

PRESBYTERIAN CHURCH of KOREA

PRESBYTERIAN CHURCH of MYANMAR

PRESBYTERIAN CHURCH of TAIWAN

HONG KONG COUNCIL of the CHURCH OF CHRIST in CHINA

PRESBYTERIAN CHURCH of MALAYSIA

PRESBYTERIAN CHURCH of SINGAPORE

NAURU CONGREGATIONAL CHURCH

KIRIBATI PROTESTANT CHURCH

CHURCH of TUVALU

CONGREGATIONAL CHRISTIAN CHURCH in SAMOA

UNITED CHURCH in PAPUA NEW GUINEA and the SOLOMON ISLANDS

PRESBYTERIAN CHURCH of NEW ZEALAND

CONGREGATIONAL UNION of NEW ZEALAND

UNITED CHURCH of JAMAICA and GRAND CAYMAN

GUYANA CONGREGATIONAL UNION

FOR WORLD MISSION

READ:　　　　Mark 1. 40 - 45

A story from Madagascar

I met this man sitting on the steps
of the capital city, Tana.
The steps are a popular thoroughfare
for they link the different levels of the French-styled town.
In order to cross from one part of the city to the next
people hurry up and down the steps.

The blind man was sitting at the top of one of the terraces.
He had a large pile of books beside him.
He took the books and following the dots with his fingers
he was able to read the text.
As people passed they stopped to watch.
It was unusual to see people reading
and very unusual to see such a large pile of books
belonging to one person.
He was reading the Bible in braille.

As soon as he was spoken to
his reading became voiced and audible.
The crowds gathered to see what was going on.
He happily continued to read from the Scriptures.
One passer-by stopped and engaged him in conversation.
He was handed the Malagasy Bible
so that he could read and then challenge the blind man.
And so the Bible study and discussion continued
on the steps of Tana.

I am told that the blind man
takes up his position each day on the steps
and reads the Bible
with whoever likes to stop for a while.

*Sheila Rudofsky: Personnel Secretary
of the United Reformed Church's World Church and
Mission Department*

Compelled

He couldn't help himself,
he had to beg,
he was so desperate
to be clean ...

> Jesus, when we cannot help ourselves
> and have to cry out,
> so anxious are we
> to be healed ...

>> you stretch out,
>> touch us,
>> free us,
>> and we are yours to command.

He couldn't help himself,
he had to tell them,
he was so delighted
to be restored ...

> Jesus, when we cannot help ourselves
> and have to shout,
> so overjoyed are we
> to be freed ...

>> you stand out
>> from the crowd
>> to remind us
>> to bring others at your command.

Jesus, when the Spirit compelled
and the people pursued you,
in the desert
there was God.

>> When the Spirit compels
>> and the people expel us,
>> in the remote places
>> help us find you.

READ: Mark 7. 24 - 30

Change is Pain.

I have been to the mountain top
And I have seen a glimpse of Africa to come.
I have seen a political cyclone emerging
Radically to halt the sting of evil,
And emancipate captive races from the shackles.

I have been to the mines,
And I have seen the gruesome scenes of agony.
I have seen migrants buried alive,
Natives losing their limbs and organs for a life time,
Sacred souls geared to permanent disability.

I have been to Winterland slums
And I have seen victims of deliberate policies,
Man and beast dying of hunger alike,
Falling apart under the dove of peace:
All in the name of Christianity.

I have been to Ethiopia
And I have seen a display of countless human corpses.
I have seen a natural episode
Conducted by nature itself
Upon defenceless and foodless human population.

Change is unknown in my ghetto.
Change is endless bucket system in Alexandra.
Change is pain in Africa.
Change is throttled by misdirected surrogates of the world.
Change of a free non racial democratic society is certain.
Revolutionary change shall set man free from bondage,
And the reigns of autocracy shall fall.

> *A musical poem written and sung by a young South African detainee.*
> *We heard him sing it in Speyer, Germany, during a 'Bread for the*
> *World' event.*

Our mission to all humankind

God of the Universe; Creator of all things;
your loving arms encompass the earth.
We shout for joy because you are our God
and we are your people.
Let us voice our praise and give thanks
for your goodness is beyond measure
and your mercy everlasting.

But we are confused and bewildered
when we realise that so many in our world
do not know of your great goodness,
do not know your loving arms.

Satellite pictures make it difficult to ignore
       the anguish of the mother with no milk for her child;
       people made homeless by war, floods or disasters;
       childhood forfeited for the pleasure of tourists
       their bodies abused and torn for a physical thrill;
       and the starving millions, deprived by others greed.

We want to turn it off,
blank out the pain and suffering.
We've done our best,
sent them our surplus food and clothes.

Suffering God, help us.
Help us to share not just the crumbs
but the food from our tables
the clothes from our backs
so that in our actions
others may see and know your love.

HEARING THE CRY OF THE POOR (1)

This Declaration by Church Action on Poverty is spread out over weeks 29, 30, 31 and 32. I include it here because during the year the Liberal Democratic Party invited me, at their conference, to share with them what the church had to say about poverty. I used this as the basis of what I had to say. (Other church representatives went to other party conferences.)

IT CANNOT BE RIGHT

- that some have to survive on less than £60 per week while others receive pay rises of £3,000 per week.

- that benefit levels are so low that loans are needed for essential items.

- that more people are begging in the street.

- that young people are living in cardboard boxes.

- that over one third of a million are homeless and the number of homeless households has nearly doubled in the last ten years.

- that hospital wards are being closed but waiting lists grow.

- that the mentally ill are discharged from hospital without adequate support.

- that children are sent home from school because they have no teachers.

- that people are demoralised by long-term unemployment and short-term job schemes.

- that for black people disadvantage is compounded by racism.

Jesus and the rich man

'He went away with a heavy heart.'

Lord, you said that you came
      with release for prisoners
      and new sight for the blind.

    Can you free the wealthy too?

Lord, I am a prisoner and I am blind,
      weighed down and manacled by all I possess;
      enslaved by the objects that dominate my life;
      trapped behind the bars
      of my insurance, my holidays, gadgets and cars.

    Can you free the wealthy too?

Lord, look on me with love
      free me, that I may see.

Lord, your people are prisoners and we are blind,
      not seeing beyond our buildings, budgets and bazaars;
      blinkered by our endless plans, our talks about doing;
      blind to the pain, hunger and emptiness
      crying out to be filled
      by your love.

    Can you free the wealthy too?

Lord, look on us with love
      free us, that we may see -

      that wealth is for giving, and life is for spending,
      that bread is for breaking and wine is for pouring;
          that your liberating love
          still waits to be shared
          in our loaves and our fishes.

    Can you free the wealthy too?

READ: Mark 12. 28 - 34

HEARING THE CRY OF THE POOR (2)

IT CANNOT BE RIGHT

- to cut taxes as an incentive to the rich but reduce incomes to spur on the poor.

- that economic growth is paid for by those excluded from its benefits.

- that public services are so seriously underfunded and the commitment of their staff so undermined.

- that local government is being weakened and public accountibility becoming more remote.

- to impose restriction in spheres such as education, broadcasting and trades union organisation that curtail democratic freedoms.

IT CANNOT BE RIGHT

- to deny our interdependence;

- to dismiss the possibility of social justice;

- to measure individual value in terms of economic success and use value for money as the yardstick for all spheres of human activity;

- to foster a self-serving individualism centred on getting, owning and consuming;

- that whole communities can be disrupted by decisions taken in distant offices or multi-national boardrooms;

- to learn from experience that market forces favour the rich and dispossess the poor and yet do nothing about it.

The Great Commandment

As sons and daughters of our nation
we ask you, God, about the law.
What is the first of the commandments?
Which is the greatest of them all?

We hear you tell us that the answer
is that the law above all others,
says that you, our God, are the one Lord,
there is no other, law or God.

Release us then, from adulation
of all the other gods and laws,
that would hold us in submission
and lead us to our destruction, and the earth's.

Free us from the worship of the power
brought by wealth and by position;
bring us instead to a condition
of gentle strength and penniless ownership of the world.

There is another law equal to this one:
Love your neighbour as yourself.
Love your sisters and your brothers
as you would wish to be loved yourselves.

So teach us, Lord to love our neighbour:
to find him and her at hunger's door,
needing clothes and shelter's warmth
and forgotten in prison by a tyrant's regime.

Lord, my God,
amidst the complexities of life,
and beneath the weight of human laws and commandments,
teach me the refreshing freedom of life
guided by your law of love.
Open my heart and mind to receive the gift of your love:
love which stands as the law above all laws.
Through him who brought your love into human flesh.

READ: Mark 5. 1 - 20; Mark 11. 27 - 33

HEARING THE CRY OF THE POOR (3)

WE BELIEVE

We believe that God, in whom we live and move and have our being,
has chosen to reveal the meaning of our human story.
God so loved this world
as to send us his Son and in him the true story
- the Kingdom that he preached -
is both revealed and made possible.
It was in proclaiming this Kingdom,
to which we are all invited
and in which the poor have a special place
that Jesus was rejected.
But through his death and resurrection - the story's climax -
the Kingdom is made present
and we are invited to celebrate and live this new reality.

We believe that when we pray
'Thy Kingom come, Thy will be done on earth',
we commit ourselves to be part of this story-in-the-making
and we bind ourselves to work for a social order
which mirrors, realises and incarnates the realities of the Kingdom.

Our human tragedy is to set our hearts
on mirages or look-alikes of the real Kingdom.
We turn God's gifts into idols
which promise life but cannot deliver it.
When we enthrone money, power, privilege and pleasure,
God's gifts become God-substitutes.

We believe that God's Spirit speaks
through the cries of the poor and the vulnerable
to expose our illusions and break their power over us;
calling us to our proper task of working for the emerging Kingdom,
restoring us to the human story's authentic theme.

What do you want with me?

'What do you want with me, Jesus?'
the spirit of evil cries out to you, as it tears a human life apart.

Jesus,
what do you want with people distracted, terrified,
        locked in their private conflict, isolated from each other?
What do you want with governments possessed by the urge for power,
        avid for arms at the cost of their people's poverty,
        forcing all minds into one strait-jacket?
What do you want with societies crazed by greed and besotted with
trivia?
Why get involved, Lord? Attend to the business of heaven, and let us
alone.

What you want, Jesus, you do:
        you confront dark powers with the power of your spirit,
        drive out evil with ringing words,
        replace it with peace and mercy.

'But', say those who hold rank,
the established authorities of all the ages,
'by what authority do you act like this?
We have our badge of office, who appointed you
to interfere with the order of things?'

The spirit of evil knows who you are
and sees you with greater clarity
than the self-righteous.
'What do you want with me, Jesus, son of the most high God?'

Throw back your question, Lord, in the teeth of our questioning.
What other power, in heaven or earth -
who else commands?

I must not evade your question.
I know what you want with me,
Jesus,
son of the most high God.

READ: Mark 9. 2 - 29

HEARING THE CRY OF THE POOR (4)

FROM FAITH TO ACTION

The true end of any social order, therefore, is to embody the Kingdom of God in human affairs. Signs of the Kingdom will be:

* when the basic needs of every child, woman and man are given priority.
* when the experience of the poor can contribute to the transformation of society and therefore to its salvation.
* when full citizenship is not dependent on wealth, race, status or educational privilege.
* when all are open and hopeful and joyful about the future and move towards it sharing the costs and benefits of social and economic change.

Two stories have been told here. One describes what is, the other what might be. It is because of the contrast between them that we believe a new social order is needed in Britain.
Christians have a contribution to make.
We seek a social vision:

* which is rooted in experience and especially in the hopes and struggles of those hurt by our society, who have been ignored and have no voice.
* which is grounded in our faith - the Good News that new life is possible - which calls the churches to be a sign and a foretaste of a new order which invites and enables us all to live in accordance with God's story.
* which is informed by the practical wisdom of those individuals and groups who try to base their lives on principles of mutual responsibility, respect and justice.
* which can generate feasible policies for the renewal of our wider society.

Height and Depth

Transfigured Christ,
you are the light
shining on through our darkness.

In you is summed up all the human meaning
of God's liberating love and promise.

If our eyes could entertain your brightness
all the time;
if we could remain on worship's heights,
adoring you,
we would be untouched
by grief, fear and illness.

But, because of your infinite love
for the whole human race,
you lead us back
into the deep, dark valleys
of anguish and despair;

where our faith,
though feeble and trembling itself.
will bring others to faith;
and where our commitment,
baulked by evil,
threatened by anxiety,
will prove your love true.

Faced with our own
and other people's troubles,
we may find ourselves hurt and depressed,
as you were in Gethsemane;

but even though we may not be aware,
you will transfigure us,
making us light for the world,
in the glory shining from the cross.

READ: Mark 6. 53 - 56; Mark 7. 31 - 38

To be wholly healthy (holy)
we should set right our relationships
with God, our family, our friends and ourselves.
Thus we become 'righteous'
(virtuous, upright, just and honest - Oxford Dictionary)
in our relationships.

To achieve this we need to be:

OPEN - capable of being wounded, hurt;
vulnerable; unguarded; non-defensive.

AVAILABLE - touchable, accessible,
willing to be interrupted.

TEACHABLE - anxious to learn;
humble and willing to listen, to change;
inviting advice.

HONEST - committed to the truth;
hating anything phoney, false,
insincere or deceitful.

We can now take this OATH
(to be Open, Available, Teachable and Honest)
and improve ourselves.
We come together in Christ and through Christ
and are able to reach out in love to our fellow humans.
Are we prepared for new relationships
as individuals and as an Association?

Dr Daleep S Mukarji, General Secretary of CMAI,
Christian Medical Association of India.

Touching God

Let me touch you, God,
even if it is only the edge of your cloak.
Sweep the light in which you are clothed,
within touch of my senses.

As I touch my children, mother, father,
husband, wife, neighbour, friend,
let me touch your love, offering healing.

As I see hungry people staring listlessly
through fly-covered faces at intrusive cameras,
let me see your hunger, seeking justice.

As I hear the dying notes of great music
and have been swept beyond myself,
let me hear you speak, demanding change.

As I smell the damp earth when grass is cut
and all the flowers of forest, field and wood,
let me catch your creating power, promising renewal.

As I taste bread and sample wine
and know that I am fed and filled with joy,
let me taste your victory, requiring sacrifice.

O God,
touching, seeing, hearing,
smelling, tasting
you:
let me
be healed,
offer justice,
changed,
renewed
and be prepared for sacrifice.

READ: Mark 10. 46 - 52

A story from New Zealand

Dr Hetty Rodenburg, a physician who, for the past six years,
has treated people with AIDS, writes:

'When I work with a patient,
I work with all four quadrants of their being
- the physical, emotional, intellectual and spiritual.
With an AIDS patient, the emotional quadrant is very important
as there is so much to cope with emotionally
- fear, rejection, guilt, sadness and loss.
This can be particularly acute for someone who is young.
Without the dreams of tomorrow,
it can be very difficult for a young person to keep on living.

AIDS patients must throw off the victim role.
Many of the people I see come from groups in society
that have stigmas attached to them.
The only way to help them get out of this victim role
is to offer them unconditional love.
Once they have experienced this,
they can learn to love themselves,
and be empowered to live and change their lives.

Because AIDS is connected with the immune system
which is our defence system,
it has a direct relationship with personal confidence.
People with HIV or AIDS must learn
to feel in control of their own lives,
to become aware of what is happening to their bodies
and be able to make choices.

Above all the person must rekindle hope in life.
Hope is the strongest medicine I use.
Hope and Love.'

Free to see

Jesus, I need you. Can you see me?
> I am lost in the mist of uncertainty.
> I cannot see you,
> too many distractions
> - people, noise, commotion -
> cut me off from you.

Jesus, I need you. Can you hear me?
> I am shocked, disturbed by my bold insistence
> but I must get close to you;
> past the obstructions
> which crowd me
> from your presence.

Jesus, I need you. Can you touch me?
> I am imprisoned, held back,
> bound by circumstances
> beyond my control;
> I can find
> no way out.

> *Yet Lord, as I hear your voice*
> *calling me in the distance*
> *I know you care.*
> *You have not passed me by!*

Help me to discard all ties
which keep me from you.
Help me to see clearly
as I did before.

Help me to follow you,
in faith and trust and love,
along whatever road
you lead me.

READ: Mark 6. 6b - 13

PRAY   To the Wind of God's Spirit
that blows where it wills, free, freedom bringing,
victor over Law, over Sin, over Death.

PRAY   To the wind of God's Spirit
locked in the heart and in the womb
of a woman of Nazareth village.

PRAY   To the wind of God's Spirit
that took hold of Jesus
to send him to preach good news to the poor
and release to the captives.

PRAY   To the wind of God's Spirit
that at Pentecost freed the apostles
from bias, self-centredness, fear,
opening wide the doors of the Upper Room,
that followers of Jesus might ever be a fellowship
open to the world,
free in the Word they speak,
crystal-clear in their witness,
unconquerable in their hope.

PRAY   To the wind of God's Spirit
that constantly banishes
new fears of the church
and consumes in flames all the authority
that serves not the needs of our brothers and sisters,
and through poverty, martyrdom thoroughly cleanses her.

PRAY   To the wind of God's Spirit
that reduces to ashes
presumption, pretence and pursuit of profit
feeding the flames of Justice and Liberation
- the fiery hearth of the kingdom.

So that we may blow strong in the Wind, my friends.

Poem by Pedro Casadaliga: used at the World Council of Churches Assembly

On a wing and a prayer

I'm tempted, Jesus,
to think you cannot mean it.
Nothing for the journey, you say,
beyond a stick and a pair of sandals.
Not even a survival kit?
At least we have each other,
and you, of course.
Is that your idea?

It's the urgency isn't it,
and trusting
that we will find you
on the way, at the open door,
in 'welcome' written in a stranger's smile?

It's not what we're used to,
this travelling light.
We organise ourselves to death,
cover all the contingencies,
secure ourselves against failure.

'My grace is sufficient'
you said that as well -
sounds like a wing and a prayer.

Can you be so sure
that all my hesitations
prove only openings for your strength?

Give me your Word,
loosen my tongue,
and let the Good News take wing.

READ: Mark 1. 35 - 39

We were all impressed
by the testimony from a Nanjing research student
relating to her contacts with a group of Communist Party members
who had had no previous contact with Christians.

She worked together with them
for a sound and video tape company
in the production of some cassette tapes
recording some Bible stories.

Their work began
before the events in Tiananmen Square
and continued during and after these momentous weeks.

From her these people learned more and more
about these Bible stories
and she answered their questions
about the inner meaning of the stories.
They questioned her also about her beliefs,
so that during the two months of making the tape
they learned more and more about Christianity.

On June 4th (1989) the same Communist Party members
felt very sad at the news of what their government had done.
They listened to the radio and the TV,
even though there was very little broadcast.
She was similarly very disappointed,
and indeed they found, as they discussed together,
that they had many feelings in common.
They told her how certain Christian concepts impressed them
because they could see that Christianity
had something to contribute to their society.

Searching for Christ

Why is it
that sometimes you seem suddenly to disappear
from the scene
leaving us empty and restless
      lost and searching?

Why is it
that you move on
not content for us to keep our faith as it has been
and our relationships fixed by the past?

Why is it
that we can't stay where we are and hold onto all
that we have built up and treasured?

You came to move us on
      to prod us into following
      to invite us on a journey
      to share with us a vision of God's kingdom.

Help us to leave behind rigid beliefs and fixed positions.
Enlarge our hearts and minds
      to discover you in new ways
      to know you through new people
      to follow you on new paths
      to share you in new situations.

Show us once more that you are there
      not for one day,   but all days;
      not for one part of life,   but the whole of life;
      not for the Church alone,   but the world in all its diversity.

Show us yourself, Christ.
Show us yourself.

READ: Mark 10. 1 - 16

It was in a church hall in North London.
They had pinned to their notice board
the 'Charter for Children in the Church':

1.   *Children are equal partners with adults in the life of the church.*

2.   *The full diet of Christian worship is for children as well as adults.*

3.   *Learning is for the whole church, adults and children.*

4.   *Fellowship is for all - each belonging meaningfully to the rest.*

5.   *Service is for children to give, as well as adults.*

6.   *The call to evangelism comes to all God's people of whatever age.*

7.   *The Holy Spirit speaks powerfully through children as well as adults.*

8.   *The discovery and development of gifts in children and adults is a key function of the church.*

9.   *As a church community we must learn to do only those things in separate age groups which we cannot in all conscience do together.*

10.   *The concept of the 'Priesthood of all Believers' includes children.*

'Has that had any effect?', I asked.

'Simply because they read that we now have two families
coming to this church, saying, "If this church takes children as
seriously as that, then this is the church for us."'

Hard Teaching

We are hard to teach Lord.
        We trap ourselves
        in rules and regulations,
        we finely distinguish
        decree nisi and absolute,
        while you strike to the heart of the matter.

Forgive the pharisee within us
and liberate us from legalism.
Help us to understand that a loving relationship is a union
which is neither made nor unmade by a court's decree.

We are hard to teach Lord.
        We place ourselves
        like protective barriers,
        we firmly distance
        you from your children,
        while you welcome and bless them.

Forgive the pompous within us
and cure us of our conceit.
Help us understand
that children are open to receive,
and ready to enter the kingdom.

Help us to learn,
        how to strengthen the separated,
        how to embrace the excluded,
        how to welcome the weak,
        how to accept all-ages.
Teach us how to combine hard heads with soft hearts.

READ: Mark 6. 14 - 29

We stand with John
who was killed by Herod
for undermining his authority with the truth.

We stand with Dietrich Bonhoeffer ,
who was killed by Hitler
for confronting his power with the gospel.

We stand with Martin Luther King
who was shot by the powers of hate
for revealing their racism.

We stand with Steve Biko
who was murdered in a police station
for revealing the reality of apartheid.

We stand with Archbishop Janani Luwum,
who died in Uganda
for speaking truth to power.

We stand with Oscar Romero,
who was shot in his own Cathedral
for confronting the powerful of El Salvador.

We stad with Chico Mendez,
who was killed in Brazil
because he wanted to save the trees.

We stand with Dorothy and Jean,
who were raped and killed on American streets
for speaking up for the poor.

We stand with countless thousands
who disappeared in South America,
for opposing the powers that be.

Power and authority

Herod could not lose face,
so John had to lose his head.

A grudging wife,
a dancing girl,
a glass or two too much
and a hasty oath before influential friends,
brought everything to a head -
John's head.
For Herod could not lose face.

Lord, the fear of loss of face
could ruin my life and bring me lasting shame.
And there are other things too.
I remember the time when ...
But that is dead and buried -
at least, I thought it was, until you came.
The only way I can face up
to the ghost of a dead responsibility
is to let it be dead and buried,
and for me to rise up above it, with you.

Lord, help me to meet my responsibilities and face my sin.
Help those with much more power and influence than I shall ever have -
the rulers of the world, high officials, and international stars -
to know how other lives depend on them,
and to live up to their first duty: to obey the truth,
despite all other pressures.
Often they will fail.
Use even their mistakes, Lord.
Remind them of the source of their authority,
and give them fresh resolve
to do your will, whatever the cost.
For you are the power behind all thrones.

READ: Mark 12. 13 - 17

Along with other visitors
we were invited to have lunch
with Kenneth Kaunda
at State House in Lusaka.

He welcomed us with a speech.
In it he said,
'It is good to see you preachers here.
You and I are in the same business.
We are in the business of trying to make the world
more like the place God wants it to be.
There is only one diference between you and me.
People like you,
preachers,
talk about it.
People like me,
politicians,
make decisions every day of our lives
which result in the world
becoming either more like, or less like,
the place God wants it to be.'

After lunch I talked with him.
I thanked him for his speech of welcome
and in particular for sharing
this understanding of his task.
He said,
'It is very difficult you know.
You will pray for me, won't you.'

I promised I would
and that I would ask people I met here
to pray for him and for others
who, like him, have difficult decisions to make
every day of their lives.

Wind and Power

Holy Spirit

>blow like the wind
>into the corners and
>corridors of power;
>challenge those in authority
>to distinguish the ways that belong to Caesar
>from the service to be offered to God.

Where politicians jostle for position and
ambition crowds out compassion

>**blow, Holy Spirit, blow!**

When scoring points off opponents becomes
more important than establishing justice

>**blow, Holy Spirit, blow!**

Where one word from the rich is more
important than all the pleas of the poor

>**blow, Holy Spirit, blow!**

When obsession with winning the next election
undermines the principles of good government

>**blow, Holy Spirit, blow!**

When political dogma replaces
commitment to people

>**blow, Holy, Spirit, blow!**

Blow like the wind and cleanse the
corners and corridors of power.

READ: Mark 4. 26 - 34

They asked me to visit mid-Wales
'for a rural experience'.
I suppose getting up at 5 a.m.
to help to milk the cows
could be called an experience!

The real experience
was meeting a genuinely rural community
and even in that brief encounter
having an opportunity to share their faith.

The highlight for me
was the invitation to lead a Harvest Festival
in the tiny village church at Hodley.
'We normally get half-a-dozen or so!', they told me.
But that night the chapel was full,
the whole village had turned out.

It was decorated with the crops
which had never seen a supermarket or corner shop:
these they had grown themselves.
There was a stook of oats standing in front of the pulpit,
its seeds at the height of the preacher's hand.
Together we considered the seed that sprouts and grows,
how, even those farmers do not know.
But grow it does.
Together we worshipped the God
who risks the future of his creation every year
on seed, tiny and insignificant,
that dies and is buried and grows again.
Together we considered
that the Kingdom of God is like this.
Together we considered that the Gospel
which is denied, corrupted, twisted and distorted,
still manages again and again to assert itself.

Seeds of the Kingdom

Mighty God
we rejoice in your reckless and extravagant love
scattered among us
and found in the mud and thorns of life.

We rejoice
that your will for us and for the world
is not one of carefully apportioned judgement
or neatly wrapped rewards.

Praise be!
Your aim and desire for all your creation
is a cup full and overflowing with good wine,
a banquet for all to share,
a harvest of full and ripe grains,
a growing tree in which all can make their nest.

Your gifts, freely offered,
are life in all its fullness,
hope in abundance,
peace that passes understanding,
love that none can measure
from which nothing can separate us.

Forgive us,
your all too sensible people,
for the ways we attempt to limit,
restrict, manipulate and allocate
your free and boundless love.

Forgive us,
your faithless people,
for ignoring the signs of your kingdom
growing in such unexpected places
and surprising ways.

Renew in us
the vision of your hope and purpose for creation
- to unite all things in Christ Jesus,
your word of grace and truth,
your love made flesh,
your seed buried to rise again.

READ: Mark 14. 12 - 21 and 27 - 31

A prayer from U.S.A.

O God, you are like a weaver-woman in our lives.
Out of the energy of the universe
you have spun each one of us
into a unique, colourful strand
with our own special hue and texture,
and have woven us together into your human family
that blankets the globe.
We admit that our own choices
have severed us from your loom of life
and created rents in the whole of our human fabric.

We have allowed ourselves to be bound
by the narrow contexts into which we were born
and now live our daily lives.
To insulate ourselves from fatigue and isolation
and to insure our own survival,
we have often refused to ask the hard questions
that need to be asked
for the sake of the well being of all people.

O weaver-woman God, open our eyes
to the mystery and power of your Spirit.
Refresh us with the light of your vision
so that we may once again
recognise the beauty and the wonder
of the specially spun thread that we are
and the splendour of the one colourful cloth of humanity.
Re-attach us to your loom
so that your vision may be made plain through us.

In the name of the Christ,
the One who was at one with all life.

Exact source unknown

Discipleship: Aspirations and Failures

Everything is prepared
>   the starched white cloth is spread
>   the silver is polished
>   the bread is broken
>   the wine poured out
>   the elders are gathered
>   the organ fades: all is quiet.

"Come to me all who are weary and heavy laden and
I will give you rest."

Let me recline in your comfortable words.
Let me enjoy the security of this pew, the peace of this place.
Let me close my eyes and forget the world outside.

>   It is good Lord to be here!

But Lord, I betray you as I receive this meal
>   and refuse your directing of my life
>   I betray you as I try to force you
>   to do my bidding.

>   I deny you as I take the tokens
>   of bread and wine as if you died for me alone.

>   I deny you when I am silent while
>   others mock you.

>   I deny you when I love only those who love me
>   when I exact an eye for an eye
>   when I refuse the one who begs.

Forgive me Lord
>   that I receive you without giving myself
>   that I accept your love with no thought
>   of passing it on.

>   **Lord have mercy.**
>   **Christ have mercy.**
>   **Lord have mercy.**

READ: Mark 4. 24 - 25

Dear heavenly Father,
send your Holy Spirit on us all, we pray,
that the Spirit may awaken us, illumine us,
encourage and give us the strength
to dare to take the small yet gigantic step,
to leave behind the comfort with which we can comfort ourselves
and to step forward into the hope that is in you.
Turn us to yourself.
Do not let us hide ourselves from you.
Do not accept it
when we try to do everything without you.
Show us how magnificent you are,
and how wonderful it is that we may trust and obey you.

This we ask also for all people:
that nations and their governments may submit to your Word
and be willing to strive for justice and peace on earth;

that through word and deed, your Word may be rightly told
to all who are poor, all who are sick, all prisoners,
all who are in distress, all those who are oppressed,
all who do not believe;
that they may hear it and understand it
and heed it as your answer to their groans and cries;

that Christians of all churches and confessions
may understand your Word with new eyes
and learn to serve it with renewed faithfulness;
that its truth may shine forth here and now
and stand firm amidst all human confusion and chaos
until at last it illumines all people and all things.

Praise be to you who in your Son, Jesus Christ,
set us free to confess and affirm always
that our hope is in you.

Karl Barth

Listen! - Pay attention! - Take note!

Listen! - Pay Attention! - Take Note!

We're listening Lord,
Our ears open to hear

Those who hear my words and believe,
will be given faith in abundance.

LISTEN!

We're listening Lord,
Our minds eager to understand

Those who hear my words and know me,
will know the Father also.

LISTEN!

We're listening Lord,
our wills ready to serve

Those who hear my words and obey,
will have the gift of eternal life.

LISTEN!

Listen! - Pay Attention! - Take Note!

Those who hear my words and will not listen,
will be made deaf to life and to love.

Those who harden their hearts against my children,
will be judged without justice or mercy.

Those who will not use the gifts I have given,
will lose even those which they have.

Lord Jesus Make us faithful in our listening,
wise in our understanding,
obedient in our serving
that we may not waste the talents and gifts that you have given to us,
but may always use them in your service, to the Glory of God.

When we were in Speyer, in Germany,
they took us round the hospital
which is run by the church.

In the chapel they took pride
in showing us the modern stained glass windows.
One of them was of Noah and his ark,
or so they said,
and I suppose it was,
for there was the boat, the dove,
and the over-arching rainbow.

But it was a little boat
and I wondered at the time
why the artist had made it so small.
It could have been,
if they had not told me different,
the boat on the lake with the disciples
to which Jesus walked and made the wind die down.

Or was it deliberate?
In the artist's mind are they the same:
God bringing peace, calm and a new beginning
with Noah, his family and the rainbow sign,
and Jesus bringing peace, calm and a new beginning
with Peter, the others and a gentle sea?

And there is another boat,
the symbol of the church,
on the sea of our chaotic times.
It is the ark carrying within it
the hope of the world to come,
for it carries within it the disciples of our Lord,
and they make slow progress against a head of wind.
But they are not alone,
for through the waves he comes.

The Defeat of Chaos

'And the Spirit of God brooded on the face of the waters.' (Gen. 1:2)

Help, Jesus! I'm afraid,
toiling and toiling and all for nothing,
and the wind's getting up, and the waves are rising
and we're going to sink.
O Lord, where are you?
Lord, I need you. I'm afraid.

Help, Jesus! We're afraid,
afraid of the swirling chaos
lying under the surface of things
where knife and syringe and bottle
are claiming their prey in the dark,
and children are used for pleasure;
and power tells its lies in high places.
O Lord, where are you?
Lord, we need you. We're afraid.

Help Jesus! I'm afraid,
afraid of that gulf of black darkness
that yawns in the centre of me;
and afraid to confront the darkness
for fear that it swallows me up,
yet all the time, waiting within me,
is a black hole of formless fear.
O Lord, where are you?
Lord, I need you. I'm afraid.

Help, Jesus! I'm sinking!
Oh, Lord, surely that can't be you -
that shape that walks on the waters
making to pass us by?
O Lord, where are you?
Lord, we're sinking. We're afraid.

'Take heart', he said, 'it is I. Don't be afraid.'
Then he climbed into the boat beside them.
And the wind dropped. (Mark 6:51)

One day we were in Witham.
They took us on their double-decker bus.
It has been so adapted
that each morning it can become
a meeting place for mother and toddler groups,
each afternoon an old peoples' day centre,
and each evening a youth club.

That evening we were on the bus
when it became a youth club.
I sat next to a couple of fourteen-year-old boys.
The youth leader had that day
written out his version of the Ten Commandments
and stuck them to one of the windows on the bus.
The paper was headed, 'God's Rules!'
Eventually the boys noticed it.

'Look at that!', said one, 'God's Rules!'

'Don't be stupid', said his friend,
'They're not God's rules, they're the bus's rules.
Look! it says "Don't swear!",
and "Do as your mother and father tell you."
They're not God's rules! They're the bus's rules!'

'Oh no!', said the first one,
'If they were the bus's rules,
it would have said "The bus's rules",
but it doesn't, it says, "God's rules!"'

So there they were, two fourteen year olds,
having theological debate
as to whether the Commandments are about
ways of men and women living together as children of God,
or whether they are simply ways
of one group in society exercising control over another.

Fall

*'Their religion is nothing but human rules
and traditions which they have memorised.' (Is.29.13)*

Jesus, are we really like that -
following in our father's footsteps
without a thought for the real meaning of things?
Do our Synods and structures so constrict us
that the heart has gone out of our message?

We have covered ourselves with cleverness
to avoid meeting your penetrating gaze;
we have filled our days with words,
fearing to hear your call.

Expose us for what we are;
cut us to the quick; challenge our conventions
and question our empty rituals.

Then lead us by the hand
in our true Father's footsteps
so, clothed in **your** righteousness,
our lives, committees and churches
become your community on earth.

READ:

Mark 14. 3 - 9

Time is too short to tell
the many thousand tales
of faith, in known and unknown saints,
through ages past;
though not perfected yet,
imagination fails
to grasp the glory they will share
with us at last.

Time is too short to scan
the breadth, length, depth and height
of perfect Love, self-emptied here,
and crucified:
all space can not contain
the life-creating light,
which floods the earth from Calvary,
in Christ who died.

Time is too short and yet,
high on the Spirit's wings,
we come with clouds of witnesses
to heal the earth;
God's love must be proclaimed
till every creature sings
the great Creator's praise, and knows
creation's worth.

For here, in time and space,
the perfect Three in One
has danced love's choreography
through death's dark ways;
Love's Covenant is made,
and Christ will drink new wine,
where great and feeble saints unite,
in deathless praise.

Written by Alan Gaunt, especially for the URC Assembly Communion Service 1991.

An Act of Repentance and Renewal for Remembrance Sunday

A man speaks.

> Who am I?
> What do you see when you look at me?
> Once labelled, "A Leper" and left alone,
> now, I am Simon,
> with Jesus as guest in my home.

A woman speaks.

> Who am I?
> What do you feel when I pour out my balm?
> Once labelled, "A Woman" and left unnamed,
> now, I am honoured
> as Jesus is touched by my love.

Women and men speak together.

> We remember the new man
> whom Jesus loved and accepted.
> We remember the woman
> by whom He was anointed.
> We let go all labels that limit our being,
> we see and we feel what we are becoming.

Leader.

> Sensitive and suffering God,
> on this day of painful remembering
> when we see and feel how wars break and wound you,
> sadly we confess to one another and to you,
> the conflict within us,
> the conflict between us,
> the conflict around us.
>
> Break open the vessels in which we confine you,
> keeping you close - for ourselves and our kind.
> Prepare us beforehand to bear your anointing.
> Pour out your passion on head, heart and mind.

READ: Mark 13. 5 - 13

Lord Holy Spirit
You blow like the wind in a thousand paddocks
Inside and outside the fences
You blow where you wish to blow.

Lord Holy Spirit,
You are the sun who shines on the little plant
You warm him gently, you give him life,
You raise him up to become a tree with many leaves.

Lord Holy Spirit,
You are the mother eagle with her young,
Holding them in peace under your feathers,
On the highest mountain you have built your nest
Above the valley, above the storms of the world,
Where no hunter ever comes.

Lord Holy Spirit,
You are the bright cloud in whom we hide,
In whom we know already that the battle has been won.
You bring us to our brother Jesus to rest our heads upon his shoulder.

Lord Holy Spirit,
You are the kind fire that does not cease to burn,
Consuming us with flames of love and peace,
Driving us out like sparks to set the world on fire.

Lord Holy Spirit,
In the love of friends you are building a new house,
Heaven is with us when you are with us.
You are singing your song in the hearts of the poor.
Guide us, wound us, heal us, bring us to the Father.

James Baxter: used at the World Council of Churches Assembly in Canberra.

Birthpangs of a New Age

Abba Father
we thank you for your Spirit, vibrant and free
brooding over creation and secretly working
through the lives of ordinary people.
Look with tender love on us your people.
who are so easily misled and so quickly betray you.
Strengthen us in our weakness
lead us in the way of Christ
and give us a taste of your kingdom of joy,
here and now.

Abba Father
we thank you for the promise of a new age
where all will live in love and laughter
and all creation will blossom in joy and delight.
Look with tender love on your world
which groans for new life and true peace.
Give hope to those battered by war, hunger or disaster.
Mend the broken relationships of family, friends and nations
and feed the life of your kingdom of peace,
here and now.

Abba Father
we thank you for your good news
and all who have proclaimed Christ down the centuries and
across the nations.
Look with tender love on your church
which strives to show your life today.
Give courage to those mocked and wounded for their faith
and strengthen their allegiance to you
and make the church in all places evidence of your kingdom of love,
here and now.

READ: Mark 13. 14 - 23

Chronic Illness

No more nice cliches or exciting insights,
No more adventure, high hopes and quick fixes,
No easy cures or comforting resolutions.

My world narrows, but ironically perspective widens.
Fighting is useless, acceptance of 'what is' becomes difficult.
Judging tomorrow by today or yesterday is futile.
Live in the now, letting go of the past and the future.

Life no longer demands, but becomes monotonously the same,
Nothing new - no new words, diagnosis or treatments,
Only reruns which seem more and more predictable.

Humbling,
Embarrassing,
Discouraging,
Vulnerable.

God's Kingdom principles make more sense now.
I am forced to receive rather than give.
No proud successes, only God's faithfulness.

Powerless,
Helpless,
A child in God's arms
Being loved tenderly and gently.

Helene Van der Werff

Desolation

Living God,
every place is hallowed ground,
where you are to be met.

Time after time, your holy places are desecrated
by human abominations.

Arrogant impostors claim the earth;
refugees lose everything and run away;
women, expecting, lose all hope;
infants die at the breast;
those exposed to cold and heat,
wish that they were dead.

There is blood-shed and torture;
there is grief and hopelessness;
all promise for the future
seems taken away;
the world come to an end!

We come with Jesus,
crucified and risen,
to plead for all your desperate children.

Your Holy Spirit brings
from within us all those deepest fears and longings,
for ourselves and all humanity,
which we dare not let surface.

Come and sanctify every place of suffering;
meet us in desolation,
and make it your delight.
Take earth's anguish to yourself
and heal it.
Hold the terrified, the defeated,
the dying and the dead,
in your eternal mother-love.

READ: Mark 13. 24 - 37

A litany for Advent

O wisdom, Holy Word of God,
who governs all creation with strong yet tender care;
come and show your people the way to salvation.

Come, Lord Jesus, come.

O sacred Lord of ancient Israel,
who showed yourself to Moses in the burning bush
and gave him the holy law in Sinai;
come stretch out your mighty hand to set us free.

Come, Lord Jesus, come.

O flower of Jesse's stem,
you have been raised up as a sign for all peoples,
rulers stand silent in your presence,
the nations bow down in worship before you;
come quickly to our aid.

Come, Lord Jesus, come.

O key of David, and sceptre of the house of Israel,
you open and no one can shut, and shut and no one can open;
come and free the captive from prison.

Come, Lord Jesus, come.

O king of all the nations, the only joy of every human heart,
keystone of the mighty arch of humankind;
come and save us whom you fashioned from the dust.

Come, Lord Jesus, come.

World Council of Churches

Stay Alert

God of time,
we don't know
what to make of all the predictions
horoscopes, forecasts and prophecies.
We are confused by the statistics,
baffled by the experts,
frightened by the extremists
who proclaim the end is near,
who foretell slump, war, and cosmic catastrophe.
Help us to make sense of the signs you provide,
and give us a deep trust in your goodness.

God of truth
we don't know
how we can keep on forgetting you.
We are distracted by trivia,
swallowed by sentiment,
hijacked by routines,
that make us forget you are near.
Forgive us, for our lack of loyalty,
and give us a deep commitment to your love.

God of love,
we don't know
how to live each moment in your presence.
We work, but forget to watch,
We serve, but are we alert?
We care, but are we prepared
for the unexpected?
Sustain our faith, hope and love,
and give us persistence to last to the end.

READ: Mark 6. 1 - 6; Mark 12. 1 - 12

In Nanjing the Amity Printing company
has been set up as a project of the Amity Foundation
in co-operation with the United Bible Societies.
It is a joint venture,
and like many such ventures,
it employs a general manager from overseas
- an American, Peter McInnis.

Since it opened in December 1987
more than three million Bibles and Testaments have been printed.
Of these about one million
are in the simplified characters now used in China.

In addition 30,000 Miao New Testaments,
20,000 Yi New Testaments,
30,000 Lisu Bibles,
20,000 Korean Reference Bibles,
and 10,000 Jingpo Bibles have been printed.
Large numbers of hymn books have also appeared,
including a special Korean hymnbook.

The number of Bibles and other publications
to be printed each year
is agreed with the government in advance
and so far every request has been granted.

The distribution of the Bibles
is only gradually being established.
Six centres have been set up recently,
but the transport and communications problems in China
are likely to impede distribution for many years to come.

Nevertheless the Bible is appearing in China in great numbers.
The Word of God is available to its people.

Synagogue and Vineyard

Lord you came to your own
and your own people would not receive you:
scorned in your own village,
killed in your own vineyard.

Look in mercy on your church,
lest we, your people who know you well,
should fail to hear the word that judges,
or hearing it, reject it
because it is too disturbing,
too radical,
too hard.

Look in your mercy on your church,
lest we, your people who know you well,
should shut the doors against the others
whom you love to draw to yourself;
because they are too different,
too difficult,
too demanding.

Look in your mercy on your church,
lest we, your people who know you well,
should fail to see that there are other places
where you can be at home;
because they are too uncomfortable,
too shocking,
too risky.

Look in your mercy on your church,
lest we, your people who know you well,
should miss your coming and your kingdom,
and find instead your vineyard
given to others,
and your hope
reposed in them.

READ:　　　　　　　Mark 1. 2 - 8

It was Christmas
and the minister asked the children
to come to the front and show him one of their presents.
A girl carried a doll.
'Tell me about it', said the minister,
'It was in the shop window
and I wanted it,
but my Mummy said it was too dear,
but I still got it.'

It is too dear,
this Christmas story,
held out to us every year.

It would be wonderful to have it:
God made man,
and sin forgiven;
angels songs,
and peace on earth;
starlit shepherds,
and power deflated.

But the price!
The witness and the death of John.
The rising hope of the twelve
crushed by the Friday crucifixion.
The carpenter nailed to the tree.
The creator transfixed by his creation.
The eternal pain of God.

It is too dear
and who would dare ask for it?
But we do not have to ask,
he is coming of his own volition.
It is too dear, but we still get it.

The Forerunner

Announce
to the world
'God is coming!'

Proclaim
the message
'The Lord is here!'

Build
new roads,
new avenues of hope
for all people.

Lord of the wild desert places,
we praise and adore you
for your refreshing message
of repentance, forgiveness,
and restoration.

Lord of the supermarket and leisure
we praise and adore you   centre,
for your blazing message
of hope, reconciliation,
and renewal.

Thank you for sending John,
as messenger - forerunner of Jesus -
to people wandering in the wilderness
of disobedience and despondency.

Thank you for sending us,
as announcers - followers of Jesus -
to people fumbling in the fog
of despair and disillusionment.

Cleanse and renew us
with your liberating love;
bathe us in your peace,
so that we are prepared
to take your Word to the world.

Set us free
with your purifying power;
inflame us with your joy,
so that we are ready
to broadcast your Word in our day.

READ: Mark 1.1.

Grassington

A poem from India

God of God...
Only the sound of an infant
crying in the night,
a familiar, homely, human sound
like the sound of hooves on flagstones,
like the rattle of chains tethering cattle,
like the crunch of straw in the mouths of oxen,
like the rustle of hay tossed into a manger.

Light of light...
Only the light of a star
falling on an infant in a crib
like the light of a shepherd's lantern,
like the light in the eys of a mother,
like the light in the learning of wise men,
like the light that lightens each dawn.

Very God of very God...
Only a pillow of straw
and an infant in rags and tatters
like the weather-worn blankets of shepherds,
like dusty, travel-stained garments of travellers,
like old cloths stuffed in a stable window
to keep the draught out and the cattle warm.

God is with us,
terribly, simply, with us.
And the shadows of men
with arms outstretched to take him
fall across the manger
in the form of a cross.

Chandran Devanesen

The Incarnation

God,
the names we give and symbols we use for you
are like wrapping paper and labels,
on our Christmas presents.

*Christmas Eve
if no one from
Hebden*

They intrigue us,
they give us clues,
they inform us and,
like young children,
we become preoccupied with them.

Help us this week to penetrate
all the layers and rediscover our gift -
> God - here in the flesh,
> a human life demonstrating eternal love,
> a first step towards the resurrection,
> the forgiving Son of God saying,
> "I love you - I accept you."

Help us to expect you for Christmas.
Break into our rituals
colour our thoughts
shape our plans.
Clasp our hand when we greet friends.
Grin at us from the kids' faces.
Kiss us at the party.
Be one of us.

*Community of
Gmss / Twesh / Keith / Hebden
Life of young & old.
Resident & visitor. (Dickinson)
Value the community, those
disappointed by lack of opportunity.
Those who serve - shops, milk, post
The lonely, limited, problems,
illness, hospital.
post
buses
health care
refreshments
other
services
The witness of the churches.
A message for the world.*

READ: Mark 2. 18 - 22

A profession of faith: the Apostle's Creed

Do you believe in God?

I believe in God,
the Father almighty,
creator of heaven and earth.

Do you believe in Jesus Christ?

I believe in Jesus Christ,
God's only Son, our Lord.
He was conceived by the power of the Holy Spirit
and born of the virgin Mary.
He suffered under Pontious Pilate,
was crucified, died and was buried.
He descended to the dead.
On the third day he rose again.
He ascended into heaven,
and is seated on the right hand of the Father.
He will come again to judge the living and the dead.

Do you believe in the Holy Spirit?

I believe in the Holy Spirit,
the holy catholic church,
the communion of saints,
the forgiveness of sins,
the resurrection of the body,
and the life everlasting.

Amen.

This is the faith of the church.

This is our faith.
We believe and trust in one God, Father, Son and Holy Spirit.

The intoxicating promise

Lord, we are weak vessels,
crude containers for your glory.
Yet we praise you
      because your power
      is radiant in weakness.

Lord, we are not worthy,
or great, by the world's standards.
Yet we praise you
      because your love
      is revealed in unworthiness.

Thank you for choosing
      weak people,
      unworthy people.
Thank you for giving us
      something to celebrate -
for filling us to the brim
with the new, invigorating wine
      of your kingdom.

Lord of new beginnings,
we praise you
      because you pour yourself out
          for us,
      you share yourself
          with us,
and give us the intoxicating promise
that we may become
new wine for the world.

A LITANY OF THANKSGIVING FOR CHINA

For the Gospel preached
>> and the Gospel heard
>> and the ready response of so many people;
for the survival of an older generation of leaders,
>> the respect in which they are held,
>> their willingness to carry the heat and burden of the day
>> even though it is time to take an evening rest;
for their lack of bitterness for horrific suffering,
>> and their willingness to make old heads think new thoughts;
for the freedom which allows
>> new churches to be opened,
>> Bibles to be printed,
>> hymns to be written;
for an illiterate woman
>> founding a village church 40 years ago
>> which now has a new building
>> built with the bricks her neighbours made,
>> and a congregation of 700;
for worship which comes from the centre of their being
>> and beats with the rythm of the human heart;
for village pastors and elders
>> with a gleam in the eye
>> which tells of hope achieved and dreams realised;
for young women and men
>> responding to the call of God,
>> listening for the Word in the words of their elders,
>> listening for the Word in the life and action of their
contemporaries,
>> listening for the Word in the mouths of strangers;
for a nation of millions
>> living in stability with each other;
for asperations expressed and questions asked
>> about mistakes which have been made
>> and corruption which has crept in;

for speeches which are made
        and authority which listens;
for intellects at work
        on the truth of the Gospel;
for medical workers
        saving the lives of mothers and babies;
for the deaf that can hear;
        the handicapped learning to walk
        and the mutes whose mouths are learning to talk;
for skilful drivers
        and thoughtful bishops;
for Buddhist mothers and Catholic Fathers
        teaching their children how to pray;
for sympathetic interpreters
        with the gift of Pentecost
        enabling all to hear in their own language:
for all these things and for so many, many more,
        I give thanks to God.